SMALL TREES

D1121090

SMALL TREES

AN ILLUSTRATED GUIDE TO VARIETIES, CULTIVATION AND CARE, WITH
STEP-BY-STEP INSTRUCTIONS AND OVER 170 INSPIRATIONAL PHOTOGRAPHS

Andrew Mikolajski

Photography by Peter Anderson

southwater

This edition is published by Southwater
an imprint of Anness Publishing Ltd
108 Great Russell Street, London WC1B 3NA
info@anness.com

www.southwaterbooks.com; www.annesspublishing.com

If you like the images in this book and would like to investigate
using them for publishing, promotions or advertising, please visit
our website www.practicalpictures.com for more information.

© Anness Publishing Ltd 2014

All rights reserved. No part of this publication may be reproduced, stored in a retrieval system,
or transmitted in any way or by any means, electronic, mechanical, photocopying, recording
or otherwise, without the prior written permission of the copyright holder.

A CIP catalogue record for this book is available from the British Library.

Publisher: Joanna Lorenz
Executive Editor: Caroline Davison
Designer: Michael Morey
Production Controller: Ben Worley

PUBLISHER'S NOTE
Although the advice and information in this book are believed to be accurate and true at the time
of going to press, neither the authors nor the publisher can accept any legal responsibility or liability
for any errors or omissions that may have been made nor for any inaccuracies nor for any loss,
harm or injury that comes about from following instructions or advice in this book.

■ HALF TITLE PAGE
Acer palmatum 'Shishi-gashira'

■ FRONTISPIECE
A weeping beech by a pond

■ TITLE PAGE
Acer

■ RIGHT
Robinia pseudoacacia 'Lace Lady'

■ OPPOSITE TOP LEFT
Prunus 'Taihaku'

■ OPPOSITE TOP RIGHT
Acer palmatum
'Roseo-marginata'

■ OPPOSITE BOTTOM LEFT
Acer palmatum 'Karaori-nishiki'

■ OPPOSITE BOTTOM RIGHT
Arbutus unedo 'Rubra'

Contents

Introduction

No garden is complete without a tree. Whether it is grown for its flowers, fruits, foliage or overall appearance, a tree will lend dignity and style to any garden, no matter how small. Even if you only have a patio, balcony or roof garden, there are trees suitable for containers. Careful selection is necessary in every case, however, particularly if you have room for only one tree: remember that a tree often outlives the gardener. This book will help you to choose from the many hundreds of trees that are available, as well as illustrating some of the most beautiful. It also offers practical advice on those trees that will best suit the prevailing conditions in your garden, and on planting, pruning and general maintenance.

■ RIGHT
In this rural English churchyard, avenues of pollarded limes, which are over a hundred years old, create a sense of peace and tranquillity.

What is a tree?

Crataegus monogyna (may or hawthorn) is a common wayside tree used to form hedgerows in northern Europe.

Trees are a large and diverse group of plants that defies precise botanical classification. What distinguishes a tree from other forms of plant life is, in fact, no more than its overall appearance. Most people understand that a tree has a single, woody trunk and a branching crown, while shrubs produce a number of stems from ground level.

Many trees, however, can develop as multi-trunked plants, while certain shrubs become tree-like on maturity. Climatic factors also play a part: some plants are unequivocally trees when growing at the foot of a mountain, for instance, but behave as shrubs at the mountain top, where strong winds will have a dwarfing effect, resulting in a thick trunk and gnarled branches. In isolation in open ground, trees will branch from ground level (or close to it) and be clothed in leaves; in forests, where the planting is denser and they are competing for light, trees will develop tall, slim trunks, branching only near the top to form the characteristic leaf canopy. Generally, trees are assumed to have a height greater than 3m (10ft), while shrubs are shorter than that. Some weeping trees have a much shorter trunk than that, however, but they are, nonetheless, never mistaken for shrubs.

Given enough room, many *Acer* (Japanese maples) develop a spreading habit and are shrub-like in form.

Willows are often planted to prevent soil erosion; hence, they are frequently found along the edge of streams and rivers.

Trees occur in a range of plant groups, and have adapted to most environments except deserts and tundra. Most belong to the largest group, the angiosperms (all flowering plants). Gymnosperms include conifers and cycads, while even the most primitive plant group, the ferns and mosses (pteridophytes), includes the tree ferns. Most trees are deciduous, shedding their leaves in the autumn and experiencing a period of dormancy over winter,

The brilliant golden yellow foliage of
Robinia pseudoacacia 'Frisia' lights up
this group of trees and shrubs.

although some are evergreen, and
in favourable climates will be more
or less permanently in growth.
Evergreens tend to be less hardy
than deciduous trees.

Trees are essential to the planet's
ecology. They store carbon dioxide
and produce oxygen, and the material
they shed – leaves and twigs – breaks
down in the soil to release nitrogen,
carbon and oxygen to feed the next
generation of plants. Their roots help
to prevent soil erosion, which is why
they are often planted in railway
cuttings and to retain the banks at the
sides of motorways. The vast amount
of water stored in a mature tree
also helps to prevent local flooding.
In addition, trees provide food and
shelter for a wide range of mammals,
birds and invertebrates.

Trees are economically important.
Some have edible fruit or nuts, and
others have bark or resin that can
be used in the pharmaceutical and
cosmetic industries. Wood can be
burned as fuel, or pulped to make
paper and fabric.

In this book, which excludes
conifers, small trees are understood to
have a height of 15m (50ft) or less,
but even this definition needs some
qualification. In many cases the final
size of a tree cannot be accurately

■ BELOW

What defines a tree is an open question. The laburnum on the
right is always classified as a tree and the viburnum on the left
as a shrub, but in this garden they are plants of comparable size.

predicted, particularly where seed-raised plants are concerned. Other trees are slow growing and, while ultimately large, will stay relatively small within the lifetime of whoever planted them. It is for these reasons that wide discrepancies concerning heights and spreads are to be found in plant dictionaries. It is also difficult to set limits on the life expectancy of a tree. Some can live to a venerable age, but others, such as *Betula pendula* (silver birch), tend to be short-lived in cultivation, so although they are potentially large, they seldom survive long enough to pose a problem in gardens.

Most trees that are grown in gardens today are either species or very closely related to naturally occurring forms. They are usually immune to the problems that beset other garden plants. A few have been extensively hybridized, however, most notably forms of *Acer palmatum* and *A. japonicum* (Japanese maples) and *Prunus* (ornamental cherries), resulting in a vast number of desirable subjects for including in the garden.

Small trees in the garden

Bearing in mind the diversity found among trees, it comes as no surprise that they can fulfil a variety of uses in the garden. If you have room for only one tree, remember that there are many with more than one season of interest. Some flowering trees, for instance, also have attractive berries that are not only a feature in their own right, but have the benefit of attracting birds and other wildlife into the garden.

You will also need to consider the impact the tree will have on the rest of the planting. Deciduous trees that cast dappled shade in summer will allow you to grow a range of shade-loving plants in the cool area at their feet, but the shade cast by evergreens, such as *Ilex* (holly) or *Quercus* (evergreen oak), will be too deep to support much other plant life.

Trees in garden design

A well-placed tree can make a garden, giving it an air of dignity and permanence. As the largest plants in the garden, they have a significant impact on the overall design. Use them as focal points or in pairs to frame a vista, or offset them against another dominant feature, such as a paved area or pool, to create balance.

■ BELOW
Coppiced *Cornus* (dogwood) lit up by the winter sun are doubly effective when they are planted next to a stretch of water.

They are also effective in isolation as a specimen in a lawn. The fact that a tree is permanently in view need not necessarily restrict your choice to evergreens, since many deciduous trees have an attractive habit even when out of leaf, or have some other redeeming feature. Magnolias, for instance, are grown primarily for their flowers, but in time they develop a candelabra-like outline that is pleasing when the branches are bare. Any weeping tree (usually recognizable by the presence of 'Pendula' as part of the plant name) is a good choice. Outstanding among these is *Pyrus salicifolia* 'Pendula' (weeping pear), which has elegant, willow-like silver leaves.

■ BELOW
Japanese maples make marvellous garden plants, either individually as specimens or, as here, in companionable groups.

In a very restricted space, choose an upright-growing variety (often with 'Fastigiata' or 'Pyramidalis' as part of the name). *Prunus* 'Amanogawa' makes a slender column of shell-pink flowers in spring. *Acer rubrum* 'Scanlon' and *Sorbus aucuparia* 'Sheerwater Seedling' are also effective.

Many of the Japanese maples (forms of *Acer japonicum* and *A. palmatum*) make good specimens, naturally developing a pleasing habit, but not all will do well in open situations, those with variegated leaves preferring the shelter of larger, overhanging trees. One of the most architectural of small trees is *Aralia elata* (Japanese angelica tree), which gives height and structure even in confined spaces.

Trees for flowers

Many trees are grown for their flowers and create a spectacular effect when mature. At the beginning of the year, *Salix* (willow) and *Corylus* (hazel) are harbingers of spring with their appealing catkins, but they must yield in splendour to the ornamental cherries (*Prunus*), a large group, many of Japanese origin and with appropriately exotic sounding names to match. Most flower in spring, but a notable exception is *Prunus* x *subhirtella* 'Autumnalis', which flowers in winter.

Equally desirable, more stately although slower growing, are the magnolias, but here you have to be careful to choose a variety that will

grow in your soil type. More rustic in their appeal and therefore better suited to a cottage garden are the delightful *Sorbus* (rowan), *Crataegus* (hawthorn) and *Malus* (crab apple). In late spring comes *Aesculus pavia* (red buckeye) with red or pink flowers, *Amelanchier lamarckii* with white flowers, and *Laburnum* x *watereri* 'Vossii' with yellow flowers.

There a few summer-flowering trees, but the group includes possibly the most spectacular of all small garden trees, *Catalpa bignonioides* (Indian bean tree), which has upright racemes of orchid-like, white flowers. Unfortunately, flowering is prolific only during a hot summer. On a hot, dry site, *Genista aetnensis* (Mount Etna broom) produces a striking cascade of scented, yellow, pea-like flowers.

■ ABOVE
The ripening fruits on this *Malus* will help to sustain the bird population throughout the winter. The fruits can also be used to make crab apple jelly.

■ LEFT
All the maples can generally be relied on to produce spectacular autumn colour.

■ RIGHT
Here, a mature *Magnolia* x *soulangeana* gives shelter in summer to *Hydrangea aspera* Villosa Group.

Fruits and berries

Many trees fruit as well as flower, sometimes creating a second period of interest that continues from late summer well into winter. *Malus* (crab apples) are among the best, and their striking red, yellow or orange fruit can also be cooked or made into jellies. *Sorbus* (rowan) also have attractive berries, and in some cases the colour changes or turns translucent as the weather gets colder.

Autumn colour

Deciduous trees will colour differently each year, depending on the season, and often the best of the display lasts no longer than a week or so. Soil type is also a factor, most trees producing their best autumn colour on acid soil. Nevertheless, this remains one of the most keenly anticipated events of the gardening calendar. One of the best recommendations for a good autumn display is *Cercidiphyllum magnificum* (syn. *C. japonicum* var. *magnificum*; Katsura tree). Not only do the leaves turn a brilliant orange, but as they fall they also give off the scent of candy-floss (cotton candy). Many of the acers produce glorious autumn tints, particularly the Japanese maples, but the amelanchiers and rowans are also usually reliable.

Stems and bark

Some trees come into their own during winter, when there are few other eye-catchers in the garden. *Prunus serrula*, for instance, has shiny mahogany-red bark, while that of *Betula utilis* var. *jacquemontii* (west Himalayan birch) is a gleaming white. Many *Cornus* (dogwood) have vivid red or yellow stems if they are cut back hard every couple of years or so. All trees grown for their winter effect should be positioned where they will be lit up by the winter sun. Coppiced dogwoods and willows are particularly effective near water, the reflection enhancing the effect.

■ LEFT
Flowering in late spring, *Laburnum* x *watereri* 'Vossii' is a delightful choice for a rural garden.

tunnel. If you do not have room for such an ambitious scheme, you could plant a pair to form an archway, perhaps to mark the start of a path or to divide one part of the garden from another area.

Coppicing and pollarding, in which all the previous season's growth is cut back hard annually, are two traditional practices which are used to maximize the amount of pliable young wood for basket weaving or wattle fence making. It is commonly done on willows, but *Cornus* (dogwood), *Tilia* (lime), *Carpinus* (hornbeam) and eucalyptus also respond well. Cutting back catalpas and paulownias annually encourages the production of larger than normal leaves. Given this treatment, they make valuable additions to the mixed border, but will not flower.

Two of the most bizarre and fascinating of all trees for the winter garden are *Salix babylonica* var. *pekinensis* 'Tortuosa' (syn. *S. matsudana* 'Tortuosa'; corkscrew willow) and *Corylus avellana* 'Contorta' (corkscrew hazel), both of which have twisted stems that are especially effective in winter flower displays.

Special effects

Some trees can be pruned or trained to show off a particular decorative feature. Laburnums, for instance, that are grown for their hanging racemes of yellow flowers, look spectacular planted in avenues and trained in successive arches to form a laburnum

Trees for wildlife

All trees attract wildlife, offering shelter for birds as well as being a source of food. Flowering trees will attract a variety of pollinating insects (beetles in the case of magnolias, honey bees in the case of limes), while fruiting trees will sustain birds throughout the winter. After the

Trees in containers

A surprising number of trees can be grown successfully in containers, and this can be a good way of growing plants not hardy enough to survive in the open garden, or that would not suit your soil type. All species of *Citrus* thrive in containers, as do other evergreens such as *Buxus* (box), *Laurus nobilis* (bay) and *Ilex* (holly).

Trees in containers can be moved around to create temporary focal points, or they can be enjoyed in winter in a cool, well-ventilated conservatory.

fruits have all been eaten, you can continue to feed the birds by hanging special feeders or pieces of coconut from tree branches. Nut trees, such as beech and hazel, have the disadvantage of attracting squirrels, which are generally considered a pest. Tree bark will harbour a wide range of beneficial insects.

■ ABOVE AND INSET RIGHT
This ancient oak would by now be an enormous specimen, had it not been regularly pollarded over the years.

Plant Directory

All the trees described here are easy to grow in fertile, well-drained soil in sun or partial shade. Any specific requirements, such as acid soil, are mentioned. They are deciduous unless otherwise stated. All can be assumed to be hardy down to -15°C (5°F) unless otherwise indicated, but remember that many trees will need protection from hard frosts when young, and are fully hardy only once established. Heights and spreads are approximate, as are growth rates, which will depend on the local climate and situation.

■ ABOVE
ACER X *CONSPICUUM* 'PHOENIX'

A rare and desirable hybrid between *Acer pensylvanicum* and *A. davidii*, grown mainly for the beauty of its green bark, which turns vivid pink, striped silver, in winter. The autumn display is also good, the leaves turning a bright golden yellow. Height 5m (16ft), spread 3m (10ft).

■ LEFT
ACER GRISEUM (PAPERBARK MAPLE)

This maple, native to China, is one of the most outstanding members of a fine genus. The leaves turn a brilliant red before they fall in autumn, but the main interest is the cinnamon-red bark, which peels to reveal a richer colour beneath. Height 5m (16ft), spread 2m (6½ft).

JAPANESE MAPLES

Cultivars of both *Acer japonicum* and *A. palmatum* are often referred to as Japanese maples. They are all outstandingly elegant and, as they are slow growing, are particularly suitable for small gardens. Most provide spectacular autumn colour (red or yellow). *A. japonicum* cultivars tend to make more airy, spreading trees; those of *A. palmatum* (of which there is a vast number) are more shrub-like, often multi-stemmed and broader than they are tall. Japanese maples are woodland plants that do best with some overhead shade; they like a leafy, fertile, but well-drained soil. *A. palmatum* cultivars are particularly susceptible to frost, which can damage the young growth, and they do best in a sheltered spot.

■ LEFT
ACER JAPONICUM 'ACONITIFOLIUM'

A slow-growing, often multi-stemmed tree or large shrub, this Japanese maple is often broader than it is tall. The soft green leaves are deeply cut and of filigree appearance. They turn vivid orange-red in autumn. Height and spread 3m (10ft).

■ ABOVE RIGHT
ACER PALMATUM F. 'ATROPURPUREUM'

A purple-leaved form of the Japanese maple, this is notable for the vibrant colours of its leaves, both when they emerge in spring and before they fall in autumn. Plants sold under this name are often raised from seed; the leaf colour as well as the final size and shape of the plant will, therefore, vary, but all make excellent garden plants. Height and spread about 3m (10ft).

■ LEFT
ACER PALMATUM VAR. *DISSECTUM*

A dome-shaped tree, with elegant, deeply cut, ferny, mid-green foliage, which turns red or yellow in autumn. It has a number of cultivars with coloured or variegated leaves. Height and spread often less than 4m (13ft).

■ LEFT

ACER PALMATUM
VAR. *DISSECTUM*
DISSECTUM
ATROPURPUREUM
GROUP

A maple with colouring
similar to that of
A. palmatum
'Atropurpureum', this
has very finely dissected
leaves, giving the plant a
more filigree appearance.
It is slow growing, and
eventually makes an
attractive, dome-shaped,
spreading tree. Height
and spread 4m (13ft).

■ ABOVE

ACER PALMATUM 'FIREGLOW'

An outstanding maple, with rich burgundy-red leaves, which turn
orange-red in autumn. It needs some sun to enhance the leaf
colour. Height and spread up to 3m (10ft).

■ ABOVE

ACER PALMATUM 'KARAORI-NISHIKI'

A rare form of Japanese maple, this has soft mid-green leaves,
which are variably splashed with cream. They turn red or yellow
in autumn. Height and spread up to 3m (10ft).

■ ABOVE

ACER PALMATUM 'KARASUGAWA'

An unusual maple, this has small, finely toothed, pinkish-red leaves, which turn bright red in autumn. Height 2m (6½ft), spread 3m (10ft).

■ ABOVE

ACER PALMATUM 'KATSURA'

This maple has palm-shaped leaves. They are pale orange-yellow when young, maturing to a rich bronze. They redden in autumn. Height 1.2m (4ft), spread 2.5m (8ft).

■ ABOVE

ACER SHIRASAWANUM 'AUREUM' (MOONGLOW MAPLE)

Although it is not strictly a Japanese maple, the moonglow maple is usefully included among them, and it is, in fact, often sold as *A. japonicum* 'Aureum'. It is a round-headed tree, with distinctive butter-yellow leaves, which turn red in autumn. This tree repays careful siting: it needs some sun to colour the foliage, but can scorch in full sun. Height and spread up to 6m (20ft).

■ LEFT

ACER PALMATUM 'SEKIMORI'

This Japanese maple is sometimes included within the Dissectum Group because of its very finely divided, filigree foliage. This is bright green, turning red or yellow in autumn. Height and spread up to 3m (10ft).

■ LEFT
ARBUTUS UNEDO F. *RUBRA*
(STRAWBERRY TREE)

The strawberry tree is an intriguing evergreen of spreading habit, which is native to south-eastern Europe and the Middle East. It produces flowers – white on the species, pink on the cultivar illustrated here – in autumn, at the same time as the fruits from the previous year ripen. These are strawberry-like in appearance (hence the tree's common name) and, although edible, are not particularly tasty. The red-brown bark, which peels in shreds, is also an attractive feature. This tree will need winter protection in cold areas. Height and spread 6m (20ft).

■ RIGHT
BETULA ALBOSINENSIS VAR. *SEPTENTRIONALIS*
(CHINESE RED BIRCH)

In a genus renowned for the beauty of its bark, this birch, which is native to west China, is outstanding for that feature. Creamy white when young, on mature specimens (15 years old and more) the bark develops a pinkish bloom and peels to reveal a mahogany-red underlayer. The oval leaves are deep green, turning to yellow in autumn and persisting on the tree until early winter. In favourable conditions this birch can exceed the dimensions given here, but only after 20 years or more. Height 10m (30ft), spread 6m (20ft).

■ RIGHT
BETULA ERMANII
(ERMAN'S BIRCH)

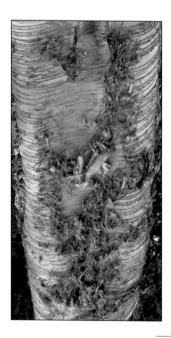

Erman's birch is native to Russia (the Kamchatka peninsula), Japan and Korea. Its garden value lies in its beautiful peeling, white bark, which is sometimes tinged with pink or cream. This feature is particularly apparent on multi-stemmed trees. 'Grayswood Hill' has pure white bark. Height 7m (23ft), spread 4m (13ft) or more.

■ RIGHT
BETULA 'FETISOWII'

An unusual hybrid of garden origin with
the characteristic peeling, chalky white
bark of the species – a strong feature in
winter. It develops a graceful, airy, narrow
crown with upright branches. The leaves
turn yellow in autumn. Height 10m (30ft),
spread 4m (13ft).

■ ABOVE
BETULA UTILIS VAR. *JACQUEMONTII*

This naturally occurring variety of the Himalayan birch
has white bark, which makes it an outstanding plant for
the winter garden. The oval leaves turn yellow in autumn.
Many of the plants sold commercially under this name
are raised from seed collected in the Himalayas, so habits
and rates of growth will vary. Selected seedlings include
'Grayswood Ghost', 'Jermyns' and 'Silver Shadow',
all of which have particularly fine bark. Height and
spread of most will not exceed 10m (30ft) in 20 years.

■ RIGHT AND INSET BELOW
CATALPA BIGNONIOIDES
(INDIAN BEAN TREE)

The Indian bean tree (which is actually from the southern
United States) gets it name from the long seedpods which
hang from the branches in autumn. Its most notable
feature, however, are the panicles of orchid-like flowers,
which are white marked with
yellow and purple-brown
(see inset). A mature catalpa
in full flower is an impressive
sight in mid-summer. The
large, soft green leaves are
also handsome, making this a
highly valued shade tree in hot
climates. Flowering is reliable
in hot summers only. Height
10m (30ft), spread 8m (26ft) or more.

■ ABOVE

CATALPA BIGNONIOIDES 'AUREA'

This selection of the Indian bean tree is less vigorous than the species and is unlikely to exceed 10m (30ft) in either direction. The soft yellow-green leaves, tinged bronze on emergence in spring, benefit from some shade from direct sun. Given that this tree is more reluctant to flower than its parent, combined with the fact that it is slightly tender, in cool climates it is best treated as a pollard or coppice and enjoyed for its leaves alone. Height and spread up to 10m (30ft).

■ ABOVE RIGHT

X *CITROFORTUNELLA MICROCARPA* (CALAMONDIN)

This is a hybrid of *Citrus* and *Fortunella*, an evergreen that produces its fragrant white flowers at the same time as the fruits from the previous season are ripening. The calamondin is hardier than most *Citrus*, and is an ideal choice for growing under glass in cold climates. Outdoors, this evergreen plant prefers neutral to slightly acid soil. Height 3m (10ft), spread 2m (6½ft).

■ ABOVE

CORNUS ALTERNIFOLIA 'ARGENTEA'

The pagoda dogwood from eastern North America, of which this is a variegated form, has a distinctive tiered habit, which makes it a striking addition to the garden, although it is slow growing and takes several years to develop its characteristic 'wedding cake' appearance. Careful staking is necessary initially to establish an upright leader. It needs acid soil. Height 2m (6½ft), spread 1.2m (4ft) or more.

■ ABOVE

CRATAEGUS LAEVIGATA 'CRIMSON CLOUD'

This hawthorn is grown for its distinctive brilliant red, white-centred flowers, which appear in late spring among the glossy, dark green leaves. Red haws, a valuable source of food for birds, ripen in autumn. Height and spread 8m (26ft).

■ RIGHT

CRATAEGUS LAEVIGATA 'PAUL'S SCARLET'

This is one of the most popular of the hawthorns, but its double, deep pink flowers, which are produced in abundance in late spring, are usually sterile, and haws are seldom produced. It is very hardy and good in exposed situations. Height and spread 8m (26ft).

■ LEFT

CRATAEGUS PEDICELLATA

This hawthorn, which is native to North America, is rarely seen in gardens. Its principal attraction is the large (for the genus), pear-shaped, red fruits, which ripen in autumn as the leaves turn orange and red. Height and spread 6m (20ft).

■ ABOVE

EUCALYPTUS PAUCIFLORA SUBSP. *NIPHOPHILA*
(SNOW GUM, ALPINE SNOW GUM)

The snow gum is valued for its brilliant, peeling, cream and grey
bark, shown to best advantage when grown as a multi-stemmed tree.
The evergreen, bluish-grey leaves are oval when young, maturing
to a sickle shape. To retain the young foliage, treat as a pollard.
Height and spread (unpollarded) 6m (20ft).

■ ABOVE

EUCRYPHIA GLUTINOSA

This slow-growing shrub or small tree is an excellent tree for acid
soil. The large, white flowers cover the plant in mid- to late summer.
In a mild climate, the tree is evergreen. In cold areas, the leaves
turn rich orange-red before falling in autumn. Height 5m (16ft),
spread 2m (6½ft) or more.

■ ABOVE AND INSET

EUCALYPTUS GUNNII (CIDER GUM)

This is one of the most versatile of garden trees. Not only can it
be allowed to develop freely as a single- or multi-stemmed tree,
but it can also be kept within bounds by hardy pruning and
grown as a shrub in a mixed border. Pruning also encourages the
ready production of young foliage, which is coin-shaped and a
gleaming pewter grey. Mature foliage is sickle shaped and has
a duller sheen (see inset). It is evergreen. Height (unless cut back)
15m (50ft), spread 6m (20ft).

■ ABOVE
MAGNOLIA SALICIFOLIA

The willow-leaved magnolia, from Japan, produces its fragrant, star-like white flowers in early to mid-spring, before the leaves, which are lemon-scented, appear. This is one of the fastest-growing magnolias. Height 10m (30ft), spread 6m (20ft).

■ ABOVE
MAGNOLIA X *SOULANGEANA* 'AMABILIS'

M. x *soulangeana* hybrids are probably the most popular of magnolias, rightly so because not only are they tough, hardy and flower freely from an early age, but they develop a pleasing habit as they mature. All have characteristic goblet-like flowers in mid-spring. The many selections have a range of flower colours, from deep rose-purple to creamy white. Those of 'Amabilis', one of the slowest growing, are pure white. Height and spread up to 6m (20ft).

■ LEFT
MAGNOLIA SPRENGERI

This slow-growing Chinese species makes a spreading tree with cup-shaped, white to pink flowers in mid-spring before the leaves appear. Height 15m (50ft), spread 10m (30ft).

■ ABOVE
MALUS 'EVERESTE'

This crab apple bears a profusion of large, white flowers in spring, opening from pink buds. The fruits, which develop in autumn as the leaves turn yellow, are bright orange to red. It will ultimately grow larger than the dimensions indicated. Height 1.5m (5ft), spread 1m (3ft).

■ LEFT
MALUS 'JOHN DOWNIE'

One of the best crab apples, and the best for making crab apple jelly, this tree bears cup-shaped, white flowers in spring. These are followed by quantities of egg-shaped, orange and red fruits. It will ultimately grow larger than the dimensions indicated. Height 1.5m (5ft), spread 1m (3ft).

■ LEFT AND INSET ABOVE
MORUS ALBA 'PENDULA'

The mulberry, a tree that is native to China, is rich in historical association, and this weeping form is an ideal variety if space is limited. The shiny, heart-shaped leaves turn yellow in autumn as the edible fruits ripen (see inset). Unfortunately, the fruits are not borne in abundance. It often grows considerably smaller than the dimensions indicated. Height and spread 4m (13ft).

■ RIGHT

NYSSA SYLVATICA (TUPELO)

This slow-growing species, which is native to China, is largely grown for its brilliant autumn colouring. The glossy leaves, bronze when young, become dark green when mature. They turn bright orange and yellow in autumn, and, on occasion, can continue to deepen in colour until they become bright scarlet. The flowers are inconspicuous, and are followed by small berries. Crowded branches should be thinned out in late winter. Height and spread 10m (30ft).

■ RIGHT AND INSET BELOW

PAULOWNIA TOMENTOSA (FOXGLOVE TREE, EMPRESS TREE)

The common name of the foxglove tree, which is native to China, derives from the upright spires of foxglove-like, mauve flowers. Unfortunately, the overwintering flower buds are generally killed by frosts in cold climates. In areas with hard winters, therefore, it is usually best enjoyed for its hairy young shoots and leaves (see inset) and cut hard back annually in early spring. Height (unless coppiced) 12m (40ft), spread 10m (30ft).

ORNAMENTAL CHERRIES

The flowering of the ornamental cherries (*Prunus* cultivars) is a keenly anticipated event in the gardening year; no other group of flowering trees produce such a weight of blossom. Many are of Japanese origin. Most flower in mid- to late spring, a notable exception being *Prunus* x *subhirtella*, which flowers from late autumn (but often only reaching its peak in early spring). Many have a second season of interest, when their foliage colours in autumn or have interesting winter bark. All will grow in any fertile, well-drained soil.

■ TOP LEFT
PRUNUS 'HILLIERI'

A spreading cherry with clusters of soft pink flowers in mid-spring. Height and spread up to 10m (30ft).

■ TOP RIGHT
PRUNUS 'PANDORA'

Ornamental cherry of spreading habit with clusters of pale pink flowers that open from deep pink buds. The leaves are tinged bronze on emergence, turning brilliant orange and red in autumn. Height 10m (30ft), spread 8m (26ft).

■ LEFT
PRUNUS
SARGENTII

The Sargent cherry occurs not only in Japan, but also in Korea and parts of Russia. It is a spreading tree with pale lilac-pink flowers in spring that are followed by cherry-like fruits that ripen glossy crimson in autumn as the leaves turn orange and red. Height and spread up to 8m (26ft) or somewhat larger.

■ ABOVE
PRUNUS 'SPIRE'

An upright, vase-shaped tree (as befits
its name) with pale pink flowers that
appear simultaneously with the leaves
in mid-spring. The foliage turns orange
and red in autumn. Height 10m (30ft),
spread 6m (20ft).

■ ABOVE RIGHT
PRUNUS X *SUBHIRTELLA*
'AUTUMNALIS' (HIGAN
CHERRY, ROSEBUD CHERRY)

The winter cherry, from Japan, is probably
the finest winter-flowering tree, with
flushes of pink-tinged, white flowers
produced throughout winter in mild spells.
The main display usually occurs right at
the end of the winter, shortly before the
spring equinox. It will ultimately grow
larger than the dimensions indicated.
Height 3m (10ft), spread 2m (6½ft).

■ RIGHT
PRUNUS X *YEDOENSIS*

The Yoshino cherry is a Japanese hybrid
with a profusion of pale pink flowers that
fade to white in early spring before the
leaves appear. A graceful tree. Height and
spread up to 8m (26ft) or more.

■ LEFT

PTEROCARYA STENOCARPA VAR. *TOMKINENSIS*
(CHINESE WING NUT)

This is a handsome, fast-growing tree for any fertile soil, and
it does particularly well near water. Once mature, it produces
greenish-yellow catkins in early summer. The glossy green leaves
turn yellow in autumn at the same time as spikes of winged
nuts (hence the common name) develop. It will ultimately
grow larger than the dimensions indicated. Height 12m (40ft),
spread 8m (26ft).

■ BELOW LEFT

ROBINIA PSEUDOACACIA 'FRISIA'

The golden-leaved form of the false acacia is one of the most
popular of all trees for small gardens, even though it can eventually
grow quite large. Unlike other yellow-leaved trees and shrubs,
it holds its colour well into summer, and makes a splendid foil
for purple-leaved shrubs. The shoots are very thorny and brittle.
Plant in any soil and in full sun for the best colour. Height 10m
(30ft), spread 5m (16ft).

■ ABOVE

SALIX INTEGRA 'HAKURO-NISHIKI'

This willow is actually a shrub, which is usually sold grafted
on to a clear stem to create a round-headed, miniature tree.
The leaves, strikingly variegated with pink and cream, keep a
good colour well into summer. It is a good choice for a container.
Height (depending on rootstock) 1.5m (5ft), spread 1m (3ft).

■ RIGHT AND INSET BELOW
SORBUS ARIA 'LUTESCENS'

This form of the whitebeam has a more conical habit than the species, and is thus better suited to small gardens. It has a number of attractions. The leaves, which are covered in creamy white hairs, are particularly brilliant as they emerge in spring. The heads of white flowers that appear in late spring (see inset) are followed by dark red berries. Height 6m (20ft), spread 4m (13ft).

■ LEFT
SORBUS CASHMIRIANA
(KASHMIR ROWAN)

This species, which is native to the western Himalayas, is a light, airy tree, with finely toothed, pinnate, greyish-green leaves. The pink-flushed flowers are followed by spherical white berries, which remain on the tree after the leaves have fallen. Height 4m (13ft), spread 3m (10ft).

■ RIGHT
SORBUS MOUGEOTII

This is an unusual small tree or shrub, native to mountainous regions of northern Europe. The broad leaves have greyish hairs on the undersides. The fruits, sometimes lightly speckled, turn red in autumn. Height 4m (13ft), spread 3m (10ft).

■ LEFT AND INSET ABOVE
SORBUS SARGENTIANA
(SARGENT'S ROWAN)

Native to south-west China, this rowan is one of the most outstanding members of the genus. The large, crimson, sticky leaf buds make a strong statement in winter, emerging as matt green, pinnate leaves, which turn brilliant orange-red in autumn. A profusion of red berries develops from the clusters of white spring flowers. Height 5m (16ft), spread 4m (13ft) or more.

■ ABOVE
SORBUS SCALARIS (SYN. *S. AUCUPARIA* VAR. *PLURIPINNATA*)

This Chinese species makes a spreading tree or large shrub. It has glossy green leaflets which turn red and purple before they fall in autumn. The white flowers, borne in late spring to early summer, are followed by red berries. Height and spread up to 10m (30ft).

■ ABOVE
SORBUS THIBETICA 'JOHN MITCHELL'

A notable selection of a Chinese species, this, like *S. aria* 'Lutescens', has leaves that are covered with white hairs on the undersides in spring, making a brilliant effect when blown by the wind. The foliage turns yellow in autumn, when the green berries ripen to red. Height 6m (20ft), spread 3m (10ft) or more.

■ ABOVE

SORBUS VILMORINII

An outstanding specimen for a small garden, the species is native to south-west China. Arching branches carry glossy green, fern-like leaves, which turn red and purple in autumn. The white flowers, produced in late spring to early summer, are succeeded by berries, which are initially red but turn to white flushed with pink as winter advances. Height and spread 5m (16ft).

■ ABOVE RIGHT

STAPHYLEA TRIFOLIA (BLADDERNUT)

This species of bladdernut, which makes a small tree or shrub, is native to the eastern United States. The finely toothed leaves have hairy undersides. The dull white flowers, which appear in spring, are followed by intriguing, inflated seedpods (hence the common name). Height and spread up to 5m (16ft).

■ RIGHT

TRACHYCARPUS FORTUNEI (CHUSAN PALM)

This is the only palm hardy enough to be grown outdoors throughout most of Britain. Its exact origins are unknown, but it is widely naturalized in China and Japan. It is grown for its stiff, pleated, fan-like leaves, and, on mature specimens, its fibrous bark. It needs a position sheltered from cold winds, and young plants should be protected with fleece from the worst winter weather. It is evergreen, and in favoured situations may grow larger than the dimensions indicated. Height 4m (13ft), spread 2.5m (8ft).

Buying trees

Trees are available mainly as container-grown plants at garden centres and nurseries, usually in 3 litre (7in) pots or larger, depending on the size of the plant. The range is usually fairly limited, so for unusual varieties it is best to contact a specialist tree nursery that operates a mail order service. Specialist nurseries will also advise on the best tree for your garden.

Forestry trees are generally sold as bare-rooted plants. They are lifted from the ground when dormant and the roots are shaken free of soil. Such plants are usually sold in bulk within the trade, and only the commonest varieties (principally native species)

■ RIGHT
Root-balled trees, their roots wrapped in hessian (burlap), are sometimes available at nurseries, but are more often potted on to lengthen their shelf life.

■ LEFT
Grafted trees are easily recognized by the grafting union near the base of the stem.

are offered. Some trees (notably palms) are also sold 'root-balled'. These are also field grown, but they are lifted with the soil still clinging to the roots. The roots are then wrapped in hessian (burlap) or some kind of string bag or wire cage. More commonly, however, root-balled trees are potted up and then sold as container-grown plants.

It is preferable to buy young plants – from three to five years old – rather than mature ones, for a number of reasons. Besides being significantly cheaper, young plants establish more quickly than older ones. Mature trees take a season or two to settle into their new homes and are often reluctant to put on fresh topgrowth;

■ BELOW
Specialist nurseries carry a wide range
of trees to choose from.

within only a few years a younger specimen will have caught up. Mature trees – which are available at only a few specialist nurseries – are worth considering only if you must have an instant effect.

Price generally depends on size. You can, however, expect to pay more for certain very rare trees, which are either more difficult to propagate or take many years to develop into a

plant of saleable size, thus requiring a an increase in investment on the part of the nursery.

Most trees sold commercially will have been grafted, and the grafting union will be clearly visible near the base of the plant. If you cannot see signs of grafting, check whether the plant has been raised from seed. Seed-raised plants can vary, depending on the genetic stability of the species.

Look for healthy plants that are growing strongly and are well-balanced, with no obvious signs of disease. If you want the tree to develop with a single trunk, check that the main stem is well established. If possible, slide the plant from its container and check the roots. They should fill the container without being congested. Ultimately, the best guarantee is to buy from a reputable nursery.

Cultivation and planting

Because trees are found throughout the world in all but the harshest habitats, it follows that there is a tree to suit every garden. It is well worth assessing the soil and aspect carefully before choosing a tree for your own garden, because not all trees are tolerant of the same conditions. A good tip is to look at trees growing wild in the vicinity, and grow one of their relatives. If you live in a built-up area, look at what is growing well in your neighbours' gardens.

Acid or alkaline?

Depending on their mineral content, soils are acid, neutral or alkaline. This is expressed in terms of the pH scale, which runs from 0 to 14, 7 signifying neutral, with lower numbers indicating acid conditions and higher numbers alkaline (limy) conditions. Most soils are slightly acid, with a pH value of around 6.5.

Many trees are indifferent to soil pH, but some are very sensitive. Lime-loving plants will generally tolerate soil acidity, but the reverse is not generally true: plants that need acid soil will not grow in alkaline conditions.

The best way to determine a soil's pH value is by means of a chemical soil-testing kit, available at garden

■ LEFT
Given appropriate attention, the tree on the right will achieve the dimensions of the one on the left about five years after planting.

centres. These are easy to use and provide reliable results. If you have a large garden, it is worth testing the soil in more than one area, as pockets of acid soil can occur in predominantly alkaline sites, and vice versa.

Soil structure

As important to plant growth as pH is the soil profile. The ideal for most trees is what is often referred to as a friable loam – that is, a moist, crumbly soil that holds moisture (and hence nutrients) well, but also allows for good drainage.

Clay soils also hold moisture well and tend to be very fertile. However, they are cold in winter and slow to warm up in spring, so the onset of fresh growth is delayed. They compact easily, and if they dry out in summer, they can set like concrete and the surface can crack.

■ BELOW
Betula pendula 'Youngii' makes a striking
centre planting in this well-stocked bed.

Light, sandy soils are easy to work, and warm up quickly in spring. They are usually low in fertility, however, since water drains away quickly. If the surface is very dust-like, valuable topsoil can be blown about in strong winds, and the soil loses its fertility.

The simplest way to test soil structure is to pick up a handful and squeeze it in your palm. If it binds together in a lump and retains the impression of your fingers, you have a clay soil. If it fails to hold together and trickles through your fingers, you have a sandy soil. Loam binds into loose crumbs and can be rubbed through your fingers, leaving your hands clean.

Improving the soil

Soil fertility can be improved by working in organic matter. Not only does this improve the nutrient level, but it also benefits the structure, improving drainage on heavy soils and moisture retention on light soils. You can further improve the drainage of heavy soils by forking in horticultural grit before planting (about 1 bucketful per square yard). If you are planting acid-loving trees, make sure that any grit you use is not based on limestone.

Soil improvers

The best soil improver of all is garden compost, which is formed from a wide range of plant remains that have been allowed to break down over a period of months. It contains the widest range of nutrients. Farmyard manure is excellent for adding bulk to the soil and is light to handle, but it must be well rotted before being added to the soil. Poultry manure is high in nitrogen. Animal manure frequently contains weed seeds that have passed through the gut of the animal. Commercial equivalents are available at garden centres, bagged up like compost for gardeners who do not have stables nearby or room to stack manure. Although they are relatively expensive, they have the advantage of being weed-free.

Hop waste and mushroom composts are sometimes available in rural areas. The latter tends to be alkaline, however, so should not be used in conjunction with acid-loving plants or on soils that are already very limy. Peat is no longer recommended for general use.

PLANTING A TREE

1 Prepare a planting area with a radius of about 50cm (20in).

2 Fork over the soil and remove all traces of perennial weeds.

3 Dig a hole about twice the depth and width of the container the tree is in.

4 Fork in organic matter, such as compost (soil mix), at the base of the hole.

5 Slide the tree from its container and place it in the centre of the hole.

6 Begin to backfill around the tree with the excavated soil.

Tree planting

Container-grown trees can be planted at any time of the year, provided the ground is not frozen or waterlogged or during a prolonged dry spell. However, most gardeners prefer to plant in spring or autumn. This allows the plant a few weeks to settle in before any lengthy period of very hot or very cold weather. Spring planting also allows the tree a full season's growth before its first

winter; on the other hand, because plant roots tend to put on a spurt of growth in autumn, planting in the latter part of the year allows the tree to develop a good root system before any fresh topgrowth is produced. Bare-root specimens should be planted during the dormant season between autumn and spring. Broadly speaking, evergreens, which tend to be slightly less hardy than deciduous trees, are best planted in spring.

Trees should be planted as soon after purchase as possible. If this is not possible because of unfavourable weather, keep them in a sheltered, frost-free place and keep them well watered until conditions in the open garden are suitable for planting.

Spend time on soil preparation and take care with planting, because this helps the tree to establish quickly and also cuts down on maintenance later on. Before planting, cultivate an area

7 Insert a stake to one side of the main stem. Here, a bamboo cane is adequate.

8 Tie the stem loosely to the cane with soft string or rubber tree ties.

9 Firm the tree in well with your hands or feet, without compacting the soil.

10 Water the tree well after planting, to help it become established.

11 Mulch with straw to conserve moisture in the soil.

to five years, depending on the growth rate of the tree. Multi-stemmed trees do not need staking.

Aftercare

Keep the tree well watered during the first growing season after planting. Water in the evening, when evaporation of moisture from the soil slows down. In hot weather in summer, you will probably need to water first thing in the morning as well. Water copiously, giving two or three watering-canfuls each time. Once the tree is established, supplementary watering should not be necessary.

Keep the area around the base of the tree weed-free, because weeds will rob the tree of available moisture and thus inhibit growth. An annual mulch of organic matter, at least 10cm (4in) deep, will help to retain soil moisture and suppress weeds. Apply the mulch in spring or autumn.

of soil of about a square metre (yard). Fork over the soil, remove all traces of weeds, as well as any large stones that can hinder root development. Fork in liberal quantities of organic matter, especially if the soil is low in nutrients.

Staking

Trees with a single straight trunk benefit from staking in the early years. Choose a stake that is roughly

the thickness of the main stem and insert it to one side on planting. For very young trees with whippy main stems, a bamboo cane is usually adequate. Loosely tie the stake to the tree with soft horticultural string or with special rubber tree ties. It is important that the ties can be loosened as the trunk thickens. The stake should come no higher than one-third of the way up the trunk. The stake can be removed after three

Growing in containers

Many trees are suitable for growing in containers, particularly those evergreens such as *Ilex* (holly), *Buxus* (box) and *Laurus nobilis* (bay) that tolerate pruning to shape. However, trees in containers need more care than those in the open garden.

Containers

Trees are heavy plants, so terracotta or stone containers provide the best ballast. Plastic pots can be used on a balcony or anywhere where weight is an issue, but make sure they are properly secured and cannot blow over easily. Wooden barrels are also suitable, provided they have been treated with a plant-friendly preservative.

Compost

Trees need good-quality compost (soil mix) that is high in nutrients, particularly since they will stay in the same container for several years. The best choice is a loam-based formula. You can replace up to one-third of the compost with leaf mould or garden compost (ideally weed-free). Coir-based composts are lighter and can also give good results, but they lose nutrients and dry out more quickly.

Watering

Trees that are grown in containers need watering every day in the summer and twice a day during hot, dry spells. Make sure that the compost is thoroughly soaked at each watering. Good drainage is vital for all plants in containers if waterlogging is to be avoided. To allow excess water to run out freely, raise the planted container on special pot feet or small bricks.

Top-dressing

To keep the compost fresh, it is necessary to replace the top layer annually. In spring, tilt the container and gently scrape away the compost to a depth of 2.5–5cm (1–2in). Replace with fresh compost.

Repotting

Most trees will outgrow their container within three to five years, after which you can either remove the plant from the container and pot it on into a larger one, or shake the roots free of soil and lightly trim them back. Wash out the container and return the plant to it, using fresh compost.

Winter protection

Because the roots of any plant in a container are above ground level, freezing in winter is always a danger,

TREES SUITABLE FOR CONTAINERS

Acacia baileyana (Cootamundra wattle)	*Dicksonia antarctica* (soft tree fern)
Acacia dealbata (mimosa)	*Fortunella japonica* (round kumquat)
Acer negundo and forms (ash-leaved maple)	*Gleditsia triacanthos* 'Sunburst' (honey locust)
Acer palmatum and forms (Japanese maple)	*Ilex aquifolium* and forms (common holly)
Buxus sempervirens (box)	*Laurus nobilis* (bay)
Chamaedorea spp.	*Olea europaea* (olive)
Chamaerops humilis (dwarf fan palm)	*Prunus* 'Amanogawa'
Cordyline australis (New Zealand cabbage palm)	*Prunus* 'Kiku-shidare-zakura'
	Robinia pseudoacacia 'Lace Lady'

PLANTING A TREE IN A CONTAINER

1 Cover the base of the container with crocks or stones to help drainage. For a lightweight alternative, use broken pieces of polystyrene (plastic foam).

2 Top the crocks with a layer of grit (or perlite or vermiculite) to about a quarter or a third of the pot's depth.

3 Begin to fill with compost (soil mix) until the container is about a third of the way full.

4 Holding it by the main stem, gently slide the tree from its container.

5 Tease out the roots from the soil ball with a hand fork or with your fingers.

6 Place the tree in the centre of the pot. Allow about 2.5cm (1in) between the top of the pot and the surface of the compost for watering. Backfill with compost.

even for plants that are supposedly fully hardy. Ideally, bring them under cover, either into an unheated conservatory or greenhouse or into a shed or garage. If the containers are simply too heavy to move, wrap them loosely in hessian (burlap). You could also use an old jumper. For evergreens, loosely cover the topgrowth with special horticultural fleece or even a length of net curtain. Remove all coverings during the day.

7 Water well and top-dress with grit to help retain moisture.

8 *(right)* Once planted, the tree can be moved around the garden.

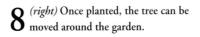

Pruning and training

Most trees are best left unpruned and allowed to develop their natural habit without intervention from the gardener, naturally achieving an elegant or imposing habit. Some have special requirements, however, or lend themselves to coppicing or pollarding – traditional techniques that were used to provide quantities of flexible shoots for basket weaving, but are now applied for their decorative effects.

The pruning of mature, established trees is best left to qualified tree surgeons who will not only own the necessary power tools but also have the expertise to use them safely. Any work on a tree that involves the use of a stepladder should be undertaken with extreme caution, to avoid accidents.

Tools

You will need a range of tools for tree pruning. Secateurs (pruners) are usually suitable for all stems of pencil thickness or thinner. Long-handled pruners are useful for reaching into the head of a tree and for attacking the base of an established coppice. A pruning saw with a serrated edge is necessary for thick branches. Evergreens can be clipped to shape with secateurs.

■ ABOVE
The lower branches of this birch tree have been removed to produce a straight stem.

Clean all tools with an oily rag after you have used them, and remember to have them sharpened on a regular basis. Blunt, rusty or dirty tools will not cut cleanly, and can damage tree bark, rendering it susceptible to disease.

Formative pruning

The only pruning that is necessary on planting is to remove any growth that may have been damaged in transit, cutting back to a healthy bud lower down. If the tree is planted as a lawn

■ ABOVE
This *Morus alba* 'Pendula' is being trained contrary to its weeping shape.

specimen and you want the grass to grow right up to the base of the trunk, the lower branches can be removed three to five years after planting, to allow access for the lawnmower.

Removing a branch

It is sometimes necessary to remove a branch from a tree, either because it is diseased or damaged. Such branches should be cut off flush with the trunk.

To minimize damage to the trunk itself, remove the branch as follows. With a pruning saw, make a shallow

■ LEFT
The dead branch
on this *Malus*
should be removed.

upward cut on the underside of the
branch about 10cm (4in) from the
trunk. Cut downwards at the same
distance to sever the branch. The
initial undercut prevents the bark
on the trunk tearing as the branch is
removed. Finally, shorten the stub.

It is no longer considered
necessary to paint the cut surface
with a wound paint or dressing.
If the tree is otherwise healthy,
the wound will rapidly callus over.

■ LEFT AND
INSET BELOW
This *Betula
pendula* (silver
birch) has been
allowed to develop
unpruned with all
its lower branches
intact (see inset).

TREES THAT CAN BE CUT BACK HARD ANNUALLY

Ailanthus altissima (tree of heaven)

Catalpa bignonioides and forms (Indian bean tree)

Cornus alba and forms

Cornus sanguinea and forms

Cornus stolonifera and forms

Corylus avellana and forms

Eucalyptus gunnii (cider gum)

Eucalyptus pauciflora subsp. *niphophila* (snow gum)

Paulownia tomentosa (foxglove tree)

Salix alba and forms

Salix exigua (coyote willow)

Salix myrsinasolia 'Nigricans'

Salix purpurea 'Nancy Saunders'

REMOVING WAYWARD GROWTH

Weeping trees

Upward-growing shoots can occasionally spoil the outline of a weeping tree. If this occurs, you will need to cut back the shoots to their point of origin as soon as you notice them.

Over time, weeping trees can develop a congested habit. In winter, when it is easier to assess the problem, thin the growth. Cut out any older branches entirely, as well as any upward-growing shoots. Shorten any branches that cross or rub against each other. In order

1 This *Fagus sylvatica* 'Purpurea Pendula' (weeping copper beech) has thrown out an upward-facing shoot that spoils the outline.

2 Cut back any such offending branch at its point of origin to maintain the tree's natural habit.

to maintain the weeping habit, cut back to a downward-facing bud. Conversely, if you wish to extend the canopy, cut back to a few well-placed,

upward-facing buds equidistant from the centre of the tree. The new growth will shoot upwards initially, but will then cascade down to form the characteristic 'curtain' of stems.

Coppicing and pollarding

There are two related techniques that can be used to enhance a particular characteristic – coppicing and pollarding. On catalpas and paulownias, the result is larger leaves. Dogwoods and willows are coppiced for their brilliant winter stems. On the debit side, trees treated in either of these ways will not flower.

■ LEFT
This weeping tree has a very congested crown that needs thinning. This job is best tackled in winter.

To coppice a tree, cut back all the stems to near ground level in late winter to early spring. The job is usually easier with long-handled pruners. Repeat the process annually or every other year. Eventually, the plant forms a woody stump (or stool) from which the new growth arises.

A pollard is effectively a coppice on a trunk. In order to form a pollard, allow the tree to develop unpruned until the trunk has reached the desired height. In late winter to early spring, cut back all the stems to within 5cm (2in) of the trunk.

To maintain the pollard, cut back all the new growth every one or two years. Remove any shoots that arise on the trunk as soon as they are seen. They will spoil the characteristic 'lollipop' shape.

■ ABOVE AND INSET
To maintain the production of young foliage on *Eucalyptus gunnii*, treat it as a coppice or pollard. The sickle-shaped mature foliage (see inset) is considered less attractive than the coin-like young growth.

■ LEFT
A coppiced tree develops a woody crown from which new shoots arise annually.

Propagation

Trees can be propagated by a variety of means. Plant nurseries usually produce their stocks by grafting, a commercial technique that reliably yields plants of saleable size very quickly. However, the rootstocks that are required for this are normally available in bulk only within the trade. The methods described below are suitable for the amateur gardener, and no specialized equipment or tools are required.

Growing from seed ensures vigorous, virus-free stock, but only seed from straight species will produce plants similar to the parent (although there can be some variation, depending on the size of the gene pool). It is possible to germinate the seeds of named varieties, but the

EXTRACTING SEED FROM LARGE FRUITS

Remove the fruits from the tree (here a crab apple) and cut them in half to expose the seeds. Gently remove them with the tip of a sharp knife (ripe seed is usually dark in colour).

resulting plants will not be identical, and can differ radically. To maintain the characteristics of the parent, propagate by cuttings.

Seed

Growing such a large plant as a tree from seed may sound rather ambitious, but it is, in fact, a very reliable method of propagation. Tree seedlings usually develop fast after germination, and it is quite possible to produce a decent-sized plant within five years. Many seed-raised trees will achieve an air of maturity within 10–15 years. Some seed can be slow to germinate, however, and needs special treatment before sowing to overcome dormancy (see panel opposite).

Seed should be sown when ripe in autumn, but it can be stored dry, in a paper bag, in the refrigerator. Most seed will germinate the following

EXTRACTING SEED FROM FLESHY BERRIES

1 Cut a spray of ripe berries from the tree (here a rowan) and squash individual fruits to release the seed.

2 Wash the seed in a bowl of lukewarm water, rubbing it between your finger and thumb.

3 Dry the seed on absorbent paper towel. The seed is then ready for sowing in pots or seed trays.

SOWING SEED

1 Prepare pots or seed trays of seed compost (soil mix), water well and allow to drain. The compost should be moist but not sodden. Lightly place the seed on the compost surface.

2 Gently press the seed into the compost. The seed should be covered to its own depth with compost. Very fine seeds should be surface-sown.

3 Lightly top-dress with grit and place in a cold frame or in a cool, sheltered spot outdoors.

spring, but some may not germinate until two years (sometimes even longer) after sowing.

Take cuttings from healthy plants only. Young trees generally supply the best material. A sharp knife is essential for all propagation work,

so that you can make clean cuts that will root quickly. Nowadays, hormone rooting compounds are now considered unnecessary.

Aftercare

When the seedlings are large enough to handle – usually when the second set of leaves appears – pot them up individually into small pots. Pot them on annually, keeping them in a cool but sheltered spot during the growing season, and overwintering them in a cold frame. Most seed-raised plants can be planted out after three to five years.

Cuttings

Taking cuttings provides a method of producing exact replicas (genetically speaking) of the parent plant. Semi-ripe cuttings are best for evergreens, whereas most deciduous trees root best from hardwood cuttings.

SPECIAL TREATMENTS

Some seed needs special treatment before sowing to accelerate or improve the chances of successful germination.

Seeds of temperate climate trees need a period of cold to break their dormancy, a process referred to as stratification. To stratify seed artificially, mix the seed with a little moist compost (soil mix) or perlite or vermiculite, and place it in a plastic bag. Seal the bag and place it in a refrigerator for six to eight weeks. The seed can then be sown as normal.

Other seeds have a thick, hard coat that naturally takes considerable time to break down. In these cases, either file down the seed coat at

one end with a nail file, or nick it with a sharp knife. Seeds of trees belonging to the pea family (Leguminosae), such as robinias and laburnums, should be put into hot water and allowed to soak for 24 hours before sowing.

Refrigerating the seed in moist compost or perlite in a plastic bag can help break dormancy and initiate germination.

Semi-ripe cuttings

From mid-summer onwards, semi-ripe cuttings can be taken as the current year's growth is beginning to firm up and become less pliable. Prepare a cuttings compost (soil mix) of equal parts peat or peat substitute and sharp sand, and use this to fill 8cm (3in) pots. Cut healthy shoots that are characteristic of the plant, cutting just above a leaf joint on the tree. Semi-ripe cuttings should be rooted by the following spring. You can test for rooting by giving each cutting a short, sharp tug. If you feel resistance, roots will have begun to form and the cuttings can be potted on individually. Cuttings that have not rooted should be returned to the pot.

Pot on the cuttings every year and keep them in a sheltered spot outdoors, until they are large enough to plant out (usually after three to five years).

SEMI-RIPE CUTTINGS

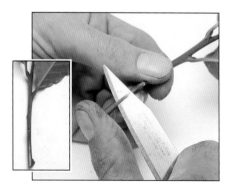

1 Take cuttings from the tree (here *Laurus nobilis* [bay]), cutting just above a leaf joint.

2 Trim each cutting at the base below a leaf joint. The cutting should be 10–15cm (4–6in) long.

3 Remove the lower leaves to expose a clear length of stem.

4 To accelerate rooting, pare away a sliver of bark about 2.5cm (1in) long at the base of the cutting.

5 Insert the cuttings into the rooting medium using a dibber.

6 Firm in the cuttings and water well. Place in a cold frame or in a sheltered position outdoors.

ROOTING HARDWOOD CUTTINGS IN THE OPEN GROUND

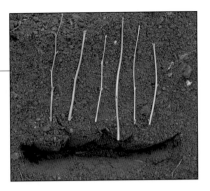

1 Prepare a trench with a spade about 20cm (8in) deep. If the soil is heavy, run a layer of grit to a depth of about 2.5cm (1in) in the base of the trench.

2 Take cuttings from the tree and trim them into lengths of up to 20cm (8in), depending on how close the buds are on the stem. Each cutting should have four or more buds.

3 Trim the base of each cutting just below a bud and the top just above a bud.

4 Insert the cuttings in the trench, making sure they are the right way up. For single-stemmed trees, insert them to their full length, so that the topmost bud is just below the soil surface. For multi-stemmed trees, two or three buds should be above ground level.

5 Firm in the cuttings using either your feet or hands.

6 Water the cuttings in well, label them and leave them undisturbed until the following autumn.

Hardwood cuttings

At the end of the growing season after leaf fall, and when the current year's growth has fully ripened, hardwood cuttings can be taken. Most will root successfully in the open ground. By altering the planting depth of the cuttings, you can control whether a single-stemmed or a multi-stemmed tree is produced.

Cut lengths of the current season's growth. Each stem will probably yield two or three cuttings, making this a very economical method of propagation.

Hardwood cuttings will take up to a year in which to root. If a heavy frost lifts them, gently firm them in again using your feet or hands. Once they have rooted, they can be grown on *in situ* for a further season or two before being transferred to their final positions in the garden.

Tree problems

Trees that are well-suited to their environment generally develop well and are free from pests and diseases, particularly species – especially if they were grown from seed. The following are some of the problems you are most likely to come across.

Epicormic shoots

How to identify Epicormic (or water) shoots are whippy stems that appear on the otherwise clear trunk of a mature tree. Sometimes they are clustered near the base. Pollarded trees are particularly prone to producing epicormic shoots.
Treatment Rub out all growth buds that arise on the trunks of trees from early spring onwards. Longer shoots should be cut back flush with the trunk with secateurs (pruners) or long-handled pruners.

Grey mould

How to identify Greyish white, fluffy mould appears on the bark of trees, generally on dead or damaged wood.
Treatment Spraying with an eco-friendly fungicide can help overcome localized problems, but you should also adopt a programme of prevention. Regularly clear away dead plant material from the base of the tree. If the tree branches are congested (resulting in poor air circulation), thin them out

or alternatively contact a qualified tree surgeon to do the job for you.

Honey fungus

How to identify Fungi appear around the base of the tree in autumn, and digging the soil reveals black 'bootlaces'.
Treatment Diseased trees should be removed and their stumps ground out by a qualified tree surgeon. Treat the soil with Armillatox to kill off the fungus.

Rabbits, hares and deer

How to identify Tree bark is gnawed. Deer will also browse tender young shoots at head

level. Young trees growing in rural areas are particularly at risk.
Treatment In a small garden, a fence is usually adequate to keep wild animals at bay. To keep out burrowing animals, sink a wire mesh barrier at least 25cm (10in) below ground level. A height of 1m (3ft) is necessary for rabbits, and 2m (6½ft) for deer. Alternatively, surround each tree with a special expanding tree guard, available from most garden centres and tree nurseries.

Reverted growth

How to identify On variegated plants, plain green shoots appear. Because they contain

Epicormic (or water) shoots commonly occur on pollarded trees, such as this lime. They can be rubbed out or cut back.

Grey mould usually appears on dead or damaged wood, such as this tree stub. Clearing away dead plant material will help.

The appearance of fungi around the base of a tree in autumn may indicate the presence of honey fungus.

The appearance of moss around the base of a tree is not a major cause for concern.

Variegated hollies sometimes produce plain cream shoots, but these do not need removing.

more chlorophyll, such shoots are always more vigorous than the typical growth, and if left untreated they can take over the tree. Occasionally, plain cream shoots arise on variegated plants, particularly on hollies, but these pose less of a threat since they contain no chlorophyll. *Treatment* Cut back all plain green growth to variegated growth that is characteristic of the tree as soon as you notice it.

Silver leaf

How to identify Leaves turn silvery grey and the shoots die back. Ornamental cherries are particularly vulnerable to it, but the disease can also spread to laburnums, willows and hawthorns.
Treatment Cut back affected growth to healthy wood as soon as you notice the problem. The disease normally enters through damaged tissue, so all pruning

of *Prunus* is best carried out around in mid-summer, when infection is least likely to occur.

Weather damage

How to identify Tree branches are felled or split. Sometimes the trunk itself is damaged. Mature trees are particularly prone to weather damage, since branches become increasingly brittle as they age. Robinias, which have

brittle stems, are especially susceptible. Strong gales can uproot entire trees. Falls of snow can also cause damage, pulling down branches. Lightning strikes are often sufficient to kill a tree.
Treatment If the damage is severe, contact a tree surgeon, who will not only tidy up damaged growth but also prune to allow the tree to regain its former balance, making it less likely to blow over. Trimming evergreens to a rough pyramid shape can prevent snow from settling in the highest branches.

Dead trees should be removed by a tree surgeon. Not only will professionals fell the tree correctly, they will also deal with the tree stump, which can rot if left in the ground.

The bark of young trees can be protected with tree guards; these will deter wild animals such as deer.

The plain green growth on this variegated maple should be cut back at the first opportunity to stop it taking over the tree.

This tree has been struck by lightning, and even if not killed outright, it is unlikely to recover fully.

Calendar

Spring

Plant new stock. Check the stakes on young trees before new growth begins and replace any that are damaged or are no longer sturdy enough to support the tree. Check semi-ripe cuttings taken the previous year for rooting. Top-dress or repot trees in containers. Take any plants overwintered under glass outdoors, but take them back under cover whenever hard frosts are forecast. Pot on seedlings and rooted cuttings. Sow seed stored over winter. Cut back all the previous year's growth on coppiced and pollarded trees. Keep a watch for epicormic shoots on pollarded trees and plain green shoots on variegated trees.

From spring onwards, rub out epicormic (or water) shoots from the trunks of pollarded trees as they arise.

Summer

Plant new stock in favourable weather. Water all newly planted trees regularly, twice a day during hot weather. Keep all trees in containers well watered and fed. Take semi-ripe cuttings of evergreens towards the end of the season. Prune any ornamental cherries that need it.

Autumn

Collect seed for sowing and either sow immediately or store in a

In late winter to early spring, cut back all the previous year's growth on coppices and pollards.

refrigerator. Plant new stock. Take hardwood cuttings from deciduous trees. Check hardwood cuttings taken the previous year for rooting. Watch out for fungal growths near the base of trees.

Winter

Firm in any hardwood cuttings that may have been lifted by frost. Prune any weeping trees that have congested heads. Protect trees that are growing in containers against harsh weather.

Check tree stakes in spring, and replace them if any are damaged.

Newly planted trees need regular watering throughout the growing season until they are established. A pipe sunk into the ground near the base of the tree will ensure that the water is carried to the roots rather than evaporating from the surface.

Plain cream leaves on holly are effective in winter flower arrangements.

Other recommended trees

As well as the trees described in the Plant Directory section, the following can also be recommended. All do well in any moderately fertile, well-drained soil, and are deciduous and fully hardy unless otherwise stated. Heights precede spreads; all dimensions are approximate.

Acacia dealbata Australian and Tasmanian species with silver-grey, fern-like leaves and masses of fragrant, fluffy yellow flowers in late winter to early spring. Evergreen. Not reliably hardy; suitable for wall-training in cold districts. 6m (20ft) x 2m (6½ft).

Acer capillipes Snake-bark maple. Erect, Japanese species with reddish young stems; the leaves open red, mature mid-green and turn crimson in autumn; the bark is striped white. 10m (30ft) x 10m (30ft).

Acer davidii Snake-bark maple. Chinese species with (usually) spreading branches. Leaves are tinged bronze on emergence and turn red and purple in autumn. The grey bark is striped white. Best in semi-shade. The selection 'George Forrest' has larger, dark green leaves but the autumn colour is not so good. 6m (20ft) x 3m (10ft).

Acer palmatum '**Dissectum Nigrum**' A Japanese maple with finely dissected blackish

Acacia dealbata

purple leaves that forms a low, rounded bush. 3m (10ft) x 4m (13ft).

Acer palmatum '**Kagiri-Nishiki**' Upright Japanese maple with leaves that have pink margins later turning cream. 3m (10ft) x 3m (10ft).

Acer palmatum '**Osakazuki**' Japanese maple with mid-green leaves that turn brilliant orange, crimson and scarlet in autumn. 5m (16ft) x 2.5m (8ft).

Acer palmatum '**Rubrum**' Japanese maple with red-tinted leaves, turning bright red in autumn. 5m (16ft) x 2.5m (8ft).

Acer rubrum '**Scanlon**' Red maple. Slow-growing, densely upright selection of a species originating from eastern North America with leaves that turn red-orange in autumn. 15m (50ft) x 5m (16ft).

Acer palmatum '**Dissectum Nigrum**'

Aesculus x *neglecta* '**Erythroblastos**' Sunrise horse chestnut. Hybrid tree with red leaf stalks and leaves that emerge cream and pink, then turn yellow before maturing green by mid-summer. 10m (30ft) x 8m (26ft).

Aesculus pavia Red buckeye. A North American species with mid-green leaves and upright panicles of bright red flowers in late spring to early summer. 3m (10ft) x 2.5m (8ft). Shrubby.

Alnus glutinosa Common alder. European species with purplish catkins in late winter and dark green leaves that emerge from sticky buds in spring. 10m (30ft) x 5m (16ft). Best in damp soil near water.

Amelanchier x *grandiflora* '**Ballerina**' Spreading hybrid with a profusion of white flowers in spring and leaves

Acer palmatum '**Osakazuki**'

that turn red and purple in autumn. 6m (20ft) x 8m (26ft).

Amelanchier lamarckii Upright shrub or small tree of unknown origin with copper red young leaves that turn orange and red in autumn; white spring flowers are succeeded by black berries. 3m (10ft) x 3m (10ft).

Aralia elata Japanese angelica tree. An east Asian species with spiny stems and coarsely toothed leaves that turn yellow, orange or purple in autumn. Panicles of white flowers are produced in late summer to autumn. 10m (30ft) x 10m (30ft).

Arbutus x *andrachnoides* Shrubby tree with peeling, reddish brown bark and small white flowers between autumn and spring. Evergreen that rarely fruits. 8m (26ft) x 8m (26ft).

Acer palmatum 'Rubrum'

Colutea arborescens

Crataegus persimilis 'Prunifolia'

Genista aetnensis

Cercidiphyllum japonicum magnificum Katsura tree. Japanese species with rounded leaves that colour yellow, orange and red in autumn and smell of toffee when they fall to the ground. Produces best autumn display in acid soil. 10m (30ft) x 8m (26ft).
Cercis siliquastrum Judas tree. South-eastern European and south-west Asian species with dark pink flowers on the bare wood in spring; kidney-shaped leaves turn yellow in autumn. 10m (30ft) x 10m (30ft).
Colutea arborescens Bladder senna. Southern European species with pale green leaves and racemes of yellow flowers, followed by green seedpods. 3m (10ft) x 3m (10ft).
Cornus 'Eddie's White Wonder' Conical tree with white flowers in late spring and leaves that turn orange,

red and purple in autumn. Needs neutral to acid soil. 6m (20ft) x 5m (16ft).
Cornus kousa Species from Japan and Korea with white flowers in summer followed by red fruits; leaves redden in autumn. This tree needs neutral to acid soil. 7m (23ft) x 5m (16ft).
Crataegus persimilis 'Prunifolia' Hawthorn of garden origin with clusters of white flowers in spring followed by bright red fruit; the leaves redden in autumn. 8m (26ft) x 10m (30ft).
Eucalyptus pauciflora subsp. *niphophila* Snow gum. Australian evergreen species with grey-green and white mottled bark and lance-shaped, blue-green leaves. 6m (20ft) x 6m (20ft).
Eucalyptus perriniana Spinning gum. Australian species with flaking, white,

green or grey bark and rounded bluish green leaves that become lance-shaped as they mature. Evergreen. Best grown as a pollard. 5.5m (18ft) x 2m (6½ft).
Genista aetnensis Mount Etna broom. Airy species from Sardinia and Sicily which has showers of golden yellow flowers in late summer that appear on virtually leafless stems. 8m (26ft) x 8m (26ft).
Ilex aquifolium 'Pendula' Weeping form of the common holly with hanging branches clothed with glossy, dark green leaves. Evergreen. 2.5m (8ft) x 3m (10ft). Other attractive weeping selections include 'Argentea Marginata Pendula', which has leaves edged silver, and 'Aurea Marginata Pendula', which has yellow-edged leaves.

x *Laburnocytisus* 'Adamii' A hybrid of *Chamaecytisus purpureus* and *Laburnum anagyroides* grafted on to a *Laburnum* rootstock. Some of the laburnum-like flowers, produced in summer, are yellow, others are purple, while a third group are purplish pink flushed yellow. All colours appear at the same time. 8m (26ft) x 6m (20ft).
Laurus nobilis Bay laurel. Evergreen Mediterranean species with glossy mid- to dark green leaves that can be used in cooking. 12m (40ft) x 10m (30ft), but can be pruned to shape.
Ligustrum lucidum Chinese privet. Evergreen species from China, Korea and Japan with oval, glossy dark green leaves and white flowers in late summer. 10m (30ft) x 10m (30ft), but can be kept smaller by regular clipping.

Magnolia 'Pickard's Schmetterling'

Mespilus germanica 'Nottingham'

Prunus 'Amanogawa'

Prunus pendula 'Stellata'

Magnolia 'Elizabeth' Conical tree with goblet-like, pale yellow flowers that appear in mid- to late spring at the same time as the leaves. 10m (30ft) x 6m (20ft).
Magnolia 'Heaven Scent' Spreading tree with goblet-like white flowers flushed deep pink outside from mid-spring to early summer. 10m (30ft) x 6m (20ft).
Magnolia 'Pickard's Schmetterling' Spreading tree with goblet-like rich pinkish purple flowers in mid-spring that open as the leaves emerge. 10m (30ft) x 6m (20ft).
Malus coronaria var. *dasycalyx* 'Charlottae' Selection of the wild sweet crab apple from North America with fragrant, semi-double pink flowers in late spring, followed by yellowish green fruits. 9m (29½ft) x 9m (29½ft).

Malus floribunda Japanese crab apple. Spreading species from Japan with pale pink flowers in late spring and small yellow fruits in autumn. 10m (30ft) x 10m (30ft).
Malus 'Golden Hornet' Rounded crab apple with pink buds that open to white flowers in late spring and are followed by bright yellow fruits. 10m (30ft) x 8m (26ft).
Malus tschonoskii Crab apple from Japan with pink-flushed white flowers in spring; fruits ripen yellow (with a red flush) in autumn as the leaves turn orange, red and purple. 12m (40ft) x 7m (23ft).
Mespilus germanica Medlar. Species from south-east Europe and south-west Asia with white flowers in late summer and rounded brown fruits (edible only after they have been frosted or

'bletted'). The leaves turn yellow-brown in autumn. 6m (20ft) x 8m (26ft).
Populus x *jackii* 'Aurora' Pillar-like tree with oval leaves splashed with white, cream and pink. 15m (50ft) x 6m (20ft), but slow growing.
Prunus 'Amanogawa' Upright ornamental cherry with usually semi-double shell pink flowers in late spring; leaves redden in autumn. 8m (26ft) x 4m (13ft).
Prunus 'Hillings Weeping' An upright tree with pendulous branches that sweep down to ground level. The white flowers appear in early spring. Up to 6m (20ft) x 5m (16ft).
Prunus 'Okame' Ornamental cherry with an abundance of carmine-pink flowers in spring, borne in clusters; the leaves turn orange and red in autumn. 10m (30ft) x 8m (26ft).

Prunus pendula 'Stellata' A selection of the Higan cherry which has star-like pale pink flowers that have a long flowering period from late autumn until the early spring. 8m (26ft) x 8m (26ft).
Prunus serrula Species originating from western China with shining mahogany-red bark that is a strong feature in the winter months. White flowers are produced in late spring; while the leaves turn yellow in autumn. 10m (30ft) x 10m (30ft).
Prunus 'Taihaku' The so-called great white cherry is one of the best-known of the group, with its dazzling white flowers in mid-spring that contrast beautifully with the emerging bronze-tinged leaves. 8m (26ft) x 10m (30ft).

Pyrus calleryana 'Chanticleer'

Pyrus elaeagnifolia

Sophora microphylla

Sorbus hupehensis

Pyrus calleryana 'Chanticleer'
Conical selection of a Chinese
species of ornamental pear,
with white flowers in spring
followed by inedible brown
fruits; leaves redden in
autumn. Eventually 15m
(50ft) x 6m (20ft), but
usually much smaller.
Pyrus elaeagnifolia Species
of ornamental pear from Asia
Minor with thorny branches
and grey-felted leaves. White
flowers in spring are followed
by green fruits. 12m (40ft)
x 8m (26ft).
Pyrus salicifolia 'Pendula'
Weeping pear. A weeping
form of a species from south-
east Europe and Asia Minor,
with willow-like, silvery
grey leaves on pendulous
branches. Creamy white
flowers appear in spring.
5m (16ft) x 4m (13ft).
Salix caprea 'Kilmarnock'
Kilmarnock willow. Weeping
tree with cascades of silvery

white catkins in late winter
on the bare wood. The leaves
are dark green. 1.5–2m
(5–6½ft) x 2m (6½ft).
Salix daphnoides 'Aglaia'
A selection of the violet
willow from Europe to central
Asia with bright red shoots
and silvery catkins before
the dark green leaves appear.
8m (26ft) x 6m (20ft).
Salix 'Erythroflexuosa'
Spreading tree with twisting
stems and leaves that are
good in flower arrangements.
Pale yellow catkins appear in
spring. 5m (16ft) x 5m (16ft),
but can be kept smaller with
regular cutting.
Sophora microphylla
Spreading evergreen species
from New Zealand and Chile
with rich yellow pea-like
flowers in mid- to late spring,
followed by dangling seed pods.
Not reliably hardy, but suitable
for wall training in cold areas.
8m (26ft) x 8m (26ft).

Sorbus aucuparia 'Sheerwater
Seedling' A narrowly upright
selection of the mountain
ash from Europe and Asia,
with white flowers in spring
followed by orange berries;
the leaves turn red or yellow
in autumn. 10m (30ft) x
5m (16ft).
Sorbus commixta 'Embley'
Selection of a species from
Korea and Japan with white
spring flowers that are
followed by an abundance of
brilliant orange-red berries at
the same time as the leaves turn
red. 10m (30ft) x 7m (23ft).
Sorbus hupehensis Hubei
rowan. Species from China,
with bluish-green leaves,
which turn red in autumn,
and white flowers in spring,
followed by white berries.
Up to 8m (26ft) x 8m (26ft).
Sorbus 'Joseph Rock' Upright
tree with white flowers in
spring followed by bright
yellow fruits in autumn as

the leaves colour brilliant
red. Susceptible to fireblight.
10m (30ft) x 7m (23ft).
Styrax japonicus Japanese
snowbell. Elegant species from
China, Korea and Japan with
fragrant, bell-shaped white
flowers in summer; the leaves
turn yellow or red in autumn.
Needs neutral to acid soil.
10m (30ft) x 8m (26ft).
Styrax obassia Fragrant
snowbell. Species from
China, Korea and Japan with
bell-shaped white flowers in
summer amid dark green leaves
that turn yellow in autumn.
Needs neutral to acid soil.
12m (40ft) x 7m (23ft).
Vitex agnus-castus Chaste
tree. Shrubby species from the
Mediterranean to central Asia
with panicles of fragrant lilac-
blue (or white) flowers in
early and mid-autumn among
dark green leaves. Needs a
sheltered spot in cold areas.
5m (16ft) x 5m (16ft).

Index

Crataegus laevigata 'Crimson Cloud'

The publisher would like
to thank the following for
allowing their photographs
to be reproduced in this
book (t=top; b=bottom;
l=left; r=right; c=centre).
Jonathan Buckley: 33t (RHS
Wisley, Surrey); 60tr (Beth
Chatto's garden, Norfolk).
The Garden Picture Library:
29bl (Didier Willery).

Sorbus sargentiana (**Sargent's rowan**)